WRITE✓STA

WRITING PROMPTS WITH

MW01121463

A SLICE
OF THE π

Laura Kay Darvill

JAMESTOWN PUBLISHERS

a division of NTC/Contemporary Publishing Group
Lincolnwood, Illinois USA

To the Teacher:

This book of mathematics prompts is geared toward the mathematics portfolio. However, several of the entries are very suitable for a writing portfolio entry. Each of these is only a suggestion and students or teachers may see items or areas that may be added or deleted. The courses listed in the Table of Contents are not all-inclusive, and many prompts could be used in additional areas.

The rubrics are also included as a recommendation and may be adapted in any assignment. Most rubrics begin with "writing focus," which is intended to cover aspects such as conveying understanding with clear and precise communication, smooth transitions, and correct grammar.

Mathematics is more than just calculations! It is hoped that this book of prompts will be useful not only as portfolio prompts but also in generating innovative ideas and projects.

ISBN: 0-89061-079-7

Published by Jamestown Publishers,
a division of NTC/Contemporary Publishing Group, Inc.
4255 West Touhy Avenue
Lincolnwood (Chicago), Illinois 60646-1975, U.S.A.

Manufactured in the United States of America

890 ML 0987654321

Table of Contents

What Does This Mean?

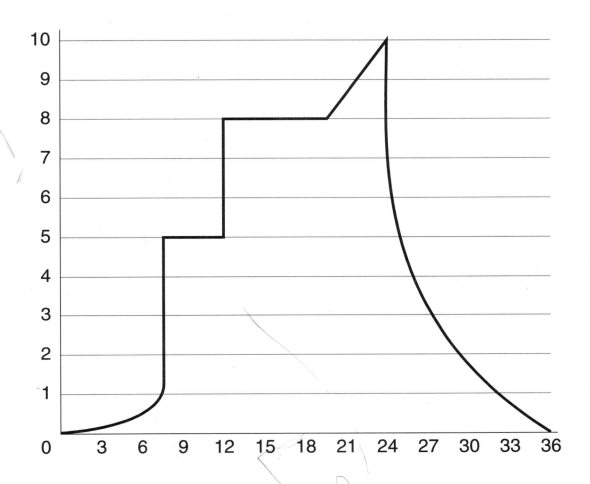

Type of Entry   Nonroutine, Writing

Concepts   Change, Mathematical Procedures (others possible)

Prompt   A graph gives a visual picture of a situation. Using the graph shown above, create a story that will be reflected in the data. You may assign any type of units for the horizontal and vertical axes.

Rubric	
Writing focus	10
Graph interpretation	10
Graph use in story	10
Creativity	10
Overall story	10
TOTAL	**50**

Define the Undefined

Type of Entry   Nonroutine, Writing

Concepts   Mathematical Procedures, Space and Dimensionality

Prompt   Most plane geometry systems contain three basic undefined terms: point, line, and plane. Most people have an intuitive idea of the meaning of each of the terms. Using your own invented words (such as *moft*, *terh*, and *quopr*), make up your own definition for each of these terms without actually using the words *point*, *line*, and *plane*. Then, using these new words, write your own definitions for *segment*, *ray*, *angles*, *parallel lines*, and *perpendicular lines*. Make up a short story using your new terms.

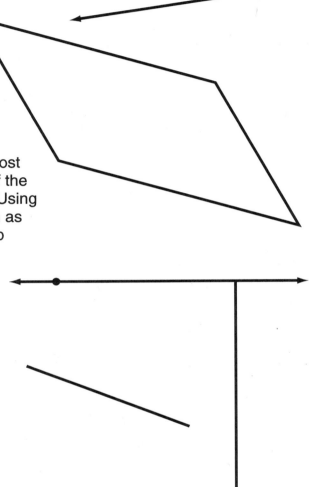

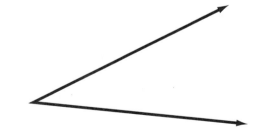

Rubric	
Writing focus	10
Creativity	10
Accuracy of definitions	10
Story	10
Mathematics in story	10
TOTAL	**50**

Name _____ Date _____

Name _____   Date _____

The Polygon Friends

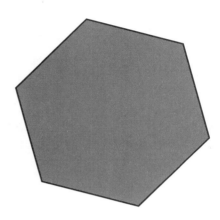

Type of Entry   Writing, Nonroutine, Project

Concepts   Space and Dimensionality

Prompt   Choose different polygons to represent you and your friends. Make up a story about yourselves, incorporating the characteristics of the polygons into it. Make a cover page, illustrate the story, and put it into a "published" form. Present the story to the rest of the class.

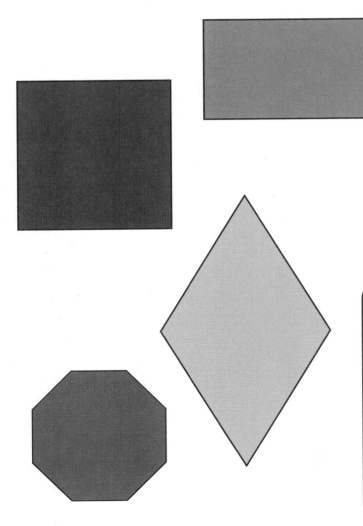

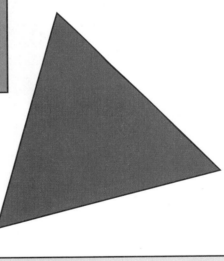

Rubric	
Writing focus	10
Cover page	10
Choice of characters	10
Use of math in story	20
Illustrations	20
Overall story	20
Presentation to class	10
TOTAL	**100**

Name _____ Date _____

_____

_____

_____

_____

_____

_____

_____

_____

_____

_____

_____

_____

_____

_____

_____

_____

_____

_____

_____

_____

_____

_____

_____

_____

_____

_____

_____

Jeopardy

graph	equation	variable	polygon	function	limit
100	100	100	100	100	100
200	200	200	200	200	200
300	300	300	300	300	300
400	400	400	400	400	400
500	500	500	500	500	500

Type of Entry   Nonroutine, Writing, Project

Concepts   Depends on the choice of categories and problems

Prompt   Make up a game of "Jeopardy" relating to the subject you are presently studying. Choose appropriate categories and questions, varying the degree of difficulty. Make a list of questions and answers, and a set of rules. As they are selected, the questions will be read aloud. After a category has been selected, cover the space with a stick-on note or erase the amount. Set up this game and play it with your class. You may use two or more teams or individual players. Players should be allowed to use paper and pencil if necessary. The game will be more challenging if some answers require working through the problem rather than using only quick recall. Provide a prize for the winner or winning team. Write a paper on the success of your game.

Rubric

Writing focus	10
List of rules	10
Choice of categories	10
Appropriate questions	20
Difficulty of questions	10
Play of game	20
Individual write-up	20
TOTAL	**100**

Name _____ Date _____

Where Do We Eat?

Type of Entry Investigation/Discovery, Application

Tools Newspaper Ads for Grocery Store and Restaurant, Menu from Restaurant

Concepts Number, Data

Prompt How do the prices of restaurant meals compare with meals cooked at home? Make a menu for a favorite dinner. After listing everything for that meal, research prices for the dinner for both a home-prepared meal and a restaurant meal. Consider the advantages and the disadvantages of eating at both places. Write a report on your findings.

Rubric	
Writing focus	10
Menu	10
Research	10
Mathematics	10
Report	10
TOTAL	**50**

Name _____   Date _____

_____

_____

_____

_____

_____

_____

_____

_____

_____

_____

_____

_____

_____

_____

_____

_____

_____

_____

_____

_____

_____

_____

_____

_____

_____

_____

Golf Shirts

Type of Entry   Application

Concepts   Number, Mathematical Procedures

Prompt   A local golf shop wishes to order shirts for the members planning to play in the Labor Day tournament. They expect to have a foursome teeing off every 10 minutes from 8:00 A.M. until 1:00 P.M., although they usually have a 4% "no-show" rate. How many shirts should they order, and how much would the shirts cost? (The price list is below.) Explain how you found the answer.

Shirts & More
Price List

12–24 . . . . $5.50*

25–36 . . . . $5.25*

37–48 . . . . $5.00*

49–60 . . . . $4.75*

Over 60 . . . . $4.50*

*per shirt

Rubric

Writing focus	10
Format of problem	10
Mathematics	10
Explanation of mathematics	10
Conclusion	10
TOTAL	**50**

The Job

Type of Entry   Application, Writing

Concepts   Number, Change, Mathematical Procedure

Prompt   As a high-school graduate, you apply for work. North Metcalfe Manufacturing Co. offers you a job with beginning wages of $10.00 an hour. If your work is satisfactory, you will receive a 10% raise after 3 months, and then another 20% raise at the end of 8 months. Sulphur Well Bottling Co. offers you a job with starting pay of $9.50 an hour. There, with satisfactory work, you will receive a 20% raise after 3 months, and another 10% after 10 months of work. You are also offered the opportunity for one day a month of overtime work at time-and-a-half. At the end of a 1-year period, which job would have paid you the most? Which job would you take and why? If you were planning to move from the area sometime within the year, how would this affect your choice of jobs?

Rubric	
Writing focus	10
Approach to problem	10
Organized calculations	10
Explanation of solution	10
Conclusion	10
TOTAL	**50**

Name _____ Date _____

How Many Caps?

Type of Entry Investigation/Discovery, Application

Concepts Number, Mathematical Procedure, Change

Prompt The F.C.A. club wished to raise money by selling "Hornet" caps. They knew that approximately 500 people were regular Hornet fans but were not sure how many people would buy their caps. Shirts & More gave them a price list on the cost per cap. Based on the price list below, how many caps should the club order and at what price should they be sold? What is the expected profit on the sale?

Shirts & More
Price List

12–36 . . . . $2.50*

37–60 . . . . $2.25*

61–96 . . . . $2.00*

Over 96 . . . . $1.80*

*each

Rubric	
Writing focus	10
Approach to problem	10
Mathematics	10
Explanation	10
Conclusion	10
TOTAL	**50**

Name _____ Date _____

20 Cubes

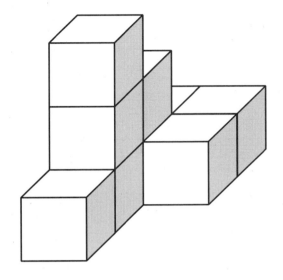

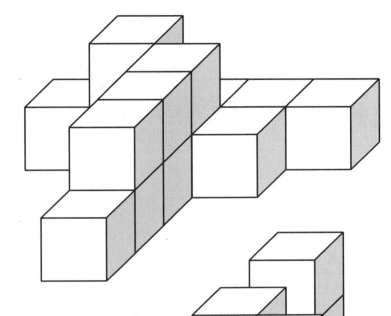

Type of Entry Investigation/Discovery, Nonroutine, Projects

Tools 20 Cubes per Person or Group

Concepts Space and Dimensionality, Change, Measurement

Prompt Use 20 cubes to build three different solids, using all 20 cubes with each solid. All of the cubes must be connected, with at least one face touching an entire face of another cube. Build each one with a different use in mind. Make a drawing of each figure and also give the surface area (including the top and base). Write a paper telling about each solid and explain how that particular shape could be used in an everyday application.

Rubric

Writing focus	10
Solids formed and drawn	10
Surface areas figured	10
Uses and explanation	20
TOTAL	**50**

Name _____ Date _____

The Charles Co.

Type of Entry Investigation/Discovery, Application

Tools Graph Paper, Ruler

Concepts Number, Change, Mathematical Procedures, Mathematical Structure

Prompt The Charles Co. manufactures and ships fishing supplies throughout the United States. For postage and handling fees, the company charges $3.00 on all orders up to $30.00 and a 10% fee on all orders over $30.00. Describe these rates algebraically and graphically. How would the percent of the fee on your order be affected if the order was under $30.00?

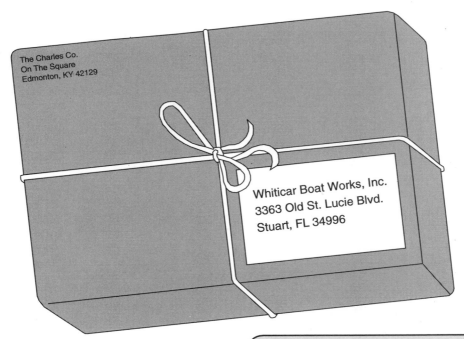

The Charles Co.
On The Square
Edmonton, KY 42129

Whiticar Boat Works, Inc.
3363 Old St. Lucie Blvd.
Stuart, FL 34996

Rubric	
Writing focus	10
Algebraic solution	10
Graph	10
Explanation	10
Conclusion	10
TOTAL	**50**

Name _____   Date _____

Larry's Rent-A-Car

Type of Entry Discovery/Investigation, Application

Tools Graphing Calculator, Graph Paper, Ruler

Concepts Number, Measurement, Change, Mathematical Procedure

Prompt Sondra wishes to rent a car for a week from Larry's Rent-A-Car. Larry gives her two options from which to choose. The Honda Prelude rents for $25.00 a day plus 20 cents a mile. The Pontiac Grand Am rents for $15.00 a day plus 25 cents a mile. Give an equation for each rate and solve the problem graphically. Which of the two options is the better deal?

Rubric	
Writing focus	10
Equation development	10
Graph	10
Explanation	10
Conclusion	10
TOTAL	**50**

Playground Equipment

Type of Entry   Application,
Nonroutine,
Project

Tools   Paper, Wire,
Straws, Glue,
Scissors, Tape,
Rulers, Markers, Other
Construction Materials

Concepts   Number, Mathematical Procedure, Space and Dimensionality,
Measurement

Prompt   You use or see many solid figures—such as prisms, spheres, pyramids,
and cylinders—daily. Work with a group to design playground equipment
for a family backyard or a park using one or more of these solids. Make a
scale drawing of the plans for your playground and for the equipment.
Make models out of paper, straws, wire, or other available materials.
Write a paper explaining
your project to the public.
Identify the solid figures
you have used. Give
approximate costs,
advantages, and
disadvantages of your
plan. Present your project
to your class.

Rubric	
Writing focus	10
Equipment design practicality	10
Equipment design creativity	10
Scale plans	20
Presentation	20
Group work during project	10
Project explanation	20
TOTAL	**100**

Name _____ Date _____

The Cereal Company

Type of Entry   Application, Nonroutine, Writing, Project

Concepts   Measurement, Space and Dimensionality

Prompt   The Summer Shade Cereal Company is creating a container for its new cereal "Summer Crunch." Although most cereal comes in rectangular boxes, the company is considering a cylindrical container as well as a rectangular box. As an engineer for the packaging company Willow Shade Wonder Boxes, you are designing two boxes from which the cereal company will choose. Design and construct a rectangular box and a cylindrical container. Design a logo and color scheme, and write information to appear on the containers. Write a paper explaining the construction of your designs and the advantages and disadvantages of each design. Draw or take a picture of the finished product. Give a presentation to the class, showing your finished product.

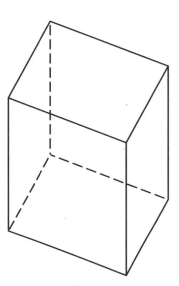

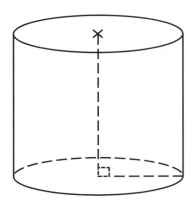

Rubric	
Writing focus	10
Scale pattern	10
Logo and design	10
Finished product	20
Picture of product	10
Written report	20
Presentation	20
TOTAL	**100**

Name _____ Date _____

Algebra Puzzle

Type of Entry   Nonroutine, Writing

Concepts   Number, Mathematical Procedures

Prompt   Danny tells Jodi, "Pick any number. Multiply the number by 3 and then add 10. Subtract the original number from the result and then divide by 2. Add 7 and then subtract your original number again. I bet I can tell you what you have left!" Jodi, knowing Danny is probably going to be right again, asks him for his guess. Sure enough, he says "12." Explain how this works, and then make up an algebra puzzle of your own.

Rubric	
Writing focus	10
Algebraic interpretation	10
Explanation	10
New puzzle	20
TOTAL	**50**

Spaghetti Break

Type of Entry   Investigation/Discovery, Project

Tools   Spaghetti (dry), Ruler

Concepts   Mathematical Procedure, Measurement, Data

Prompt   Using dry spaghetti of uniform length, ask at least 40 persons to break one strand of spaghetti into two pieces. Record the length of the larger of the two pieces. Make a tally of your information. Display the information in at least two different forms. Determine central tendencies using your data. Interpret the information. How could you use this information?

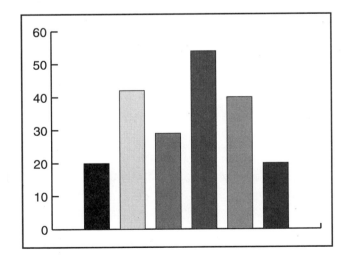

Rubric	
Writing focus	10
Tally and graphs	10
Central tendencies	10
Interpretation	10
Use of information	10
TOTAL	**50**

Job Choice

Type of Entry   Application,
Investigation/Discovery,
Writing

Tools   Graphing Calculator or
Computer (optional)

Concepts   Number, Data

Prompt   Michael has been hired by the Edmonton Chamber of Commerce to
analyze and promote the job market in Metcalfe County. He has collected
information about the pay rate of employees not in a management position
at two local factories. He has learned that the following hourly wages are
being paid to employees as listed at the present time:

Subtle Sewing Factory: $4.35, 4.60, 5.50, 5.00, 16.00, 9.50, 5.50, 4.80, 12.00, 4.35, 4.50,
5.50, 6.00, 4.35, 4.50, 14.00, 6.00, 6.00, 6.00, 4.35, 14.00, 12.00, 4.35, 4.50, 4.50, 5.00,
9.50, 6.00, 5.50, 6.00, 4.35, 4.60, 4.35, 9.50, 14.00, 4.60, 4.35, 4.60, 4.60, 4.80, 16.00, 5.50,
4.35, 4.35, 5.00, 4.80, 4.80, 12.00, 6.00, 6.00, 6.00, 4.80, 4.35, 4.60, 6.00, 14.00, 6.00, 4.35,
4.60, 6.00, 4.35, 6.00, 4.60

Salt Lick Packaging Company: $4.35, 5.00, 10.00, 13.00, 4.50, 6.00, 12.00, 4.35, 4.50,
13.00, 6.00, 5.50, 5.50, 4.75, 4.35, 15.00, 4.75, 8.00, 10.00, 12.00, 8.00, 4.50, 5.00, 6.00,
8.00, 15.00, 4.35, 4.50, 4.75, 5.00, 8.00, 6.00, 4.75, 4.75, 10.00, 6.00, 5.50, 6.00, 6.00,
12.00, 5.50, 5.00, 5.50, 6.00, 5.50, 6.00, 13.00, 6.00

Using this information about each factory and
your knowledge of statistical analysis, write up
a report with recommendations that Michael
might make about the job market in Metcalfe
County. Include charts, data, and graphs in
your report.

Rubric	
Writing focus	10
Organizing data	10
Comparing data (Charts and graphs)	20
Analyzing data (Central tendencies, etc.)	30
Recommendations	20
Grammar, structure, etc.	10
TOTAL	**100**

Free Toothpaste

Type of Entry Application, Writing

Concepts Number, Change, Measurement, Data

Prompt Willis has been hired to set up a sample test for a new brand of toothpaste, "Squeaky Clean." The community he has chosen to use for the test has approximately 10,000 persons. He has small samples of the toothpaste from the Randolph Toothpaste Company. The samples cost $0.15 each, and he can hire one person to help him at $5.50 per hour. The company has allowed him $300 for expenses, not including his own time. Set up a plan for the sample test. Determine how and where the product would be distributed, how the results would be gathered, and how the data would be used.

Rubric	
Writing focus	10
Plan for cost	20
Plan for distribution	10
Plan for gathering results	10
Use of data	20
Overall write-up	20
Conclusion	10
TOTAL	**100**

Construction Project

Type of Entry   Investigation/Discovery

Tools   Compass, Straightedge

Concepts   Space and Dimensionality

Prompt   Using a compass and a straightedge, construct the following figure. Explain your construction.

Construction   Draw a scalene triangle near the middle of your paper. Do not make your triangle too small (each side no less than approximately 5 centimeters in length). Construct three equilateral triangles, using each side of your triangle as a base. Find the center of each of the equilateral triangles by construction. Connect the centers of the equilateral triangles to form another triangle. Color or shade your new triangle. What do you observe about this triangle?

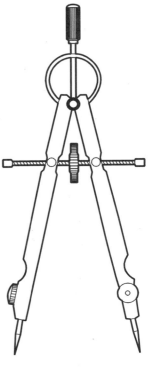

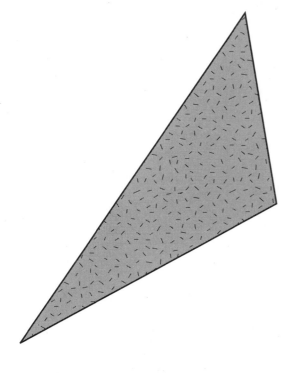

Rubric	
Writing focus	10
Construction of triangles	10
Finished construction	10
Explanation of construction	10
Observations	10
TOTAL	**50**

Circle Dissection

Type of Entry   Investigation/Discovery

Tools   Compass, Ruler

Concepts   Space and Dimensionality,
Change, Mathematical Structure

Prompt   On several circles, locate a
different number of points. In each
circle draw in all possible chords,
dividing the circle into regions.
Investigate to determine a pattern
between the number of points and the
number of regions. If a pattern exists, determine
a formula relating the number of points and regions.

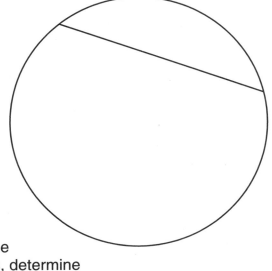

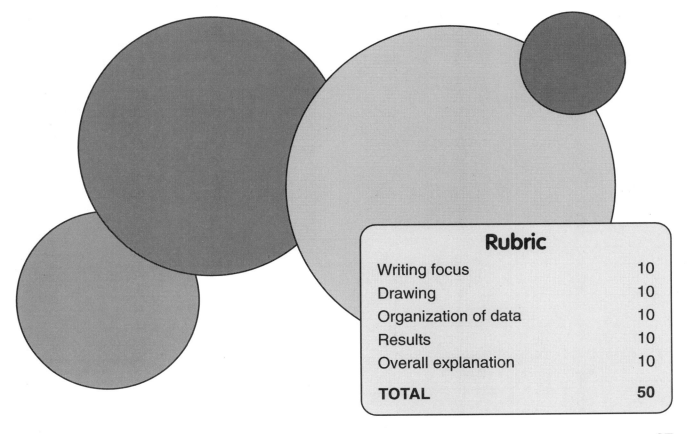

Rubric	
Writing focus	10
Drawing	10
Organization of data	10
Results	10
Overall explanation	10
TOTAL	**50**

Name _____ Date _____

Circling Around

Type of Entry   Investigation/Discovery

Concepts   Space and Dimensionality,
Measurement, Change

Prompt   Four circles are tangent to each other
and to a central circle, as shown. The
diameter of the smaller outside
circles is one unit, and the diameter
of the larger outside circles is two
units. Determine the diameter of the
inside circle. How would this change if
all the circles were the same in
diameter?

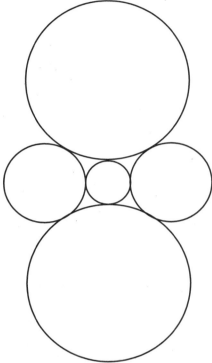

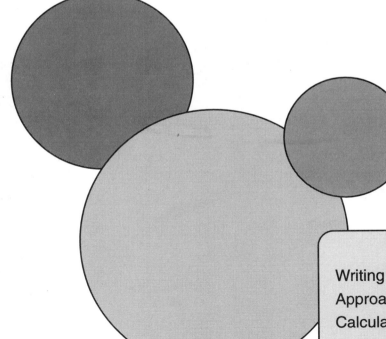

Rubric	
Writing focus	10
Approach to problem	10
Calculation process	10
Explanation and answer	10
Same-diameter discussion	10
TOTAL	**50**

© NTC/Contemporary Publishing Group, Inc.

The Midpoint

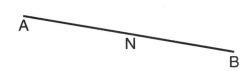

Type of Entry   Investigation/Discovery, Writing

Tools   Ruler

Concepts   Number, Measurement, Space and
Dimensionality, Mathematical Procedure

Prompt   Draw a number line and name at least 10 points on the line. Then choose
10 different segments and record the information in the chart below. After
recording your information, examine the data and determine a formula for
finding the midpoint of a segment if the coordinates of the endpoints are
known. Also, determine a formula for finding one of the endpoints if the
coordinates of the midpoint and one endpoint are known. Explain how you
arrived at your formulas.

Coordinates			
Segment	Endpoint	Endpoint	Midpoint

Rubric

Writing focus	10
Number line	10
Chart	10
Formula development	10
Conclusion	10
TOTAL	**50**

Circle/Triangle

Type of Entry   Investigation/Discovery, Writing

Tools   Compass, Ruler

Concepts   Number, Space and Dimensionality, Mathematical Structure, Measurement

Prompt   Construct a right triangle and using each side as a diameter, construct semicircles on each side. Label the sides of the triangle as a, b, and c, with c being the hypotenuse. Find the length of the sides and then find the areas of the semicircles. Compare the areas and find a relationship between them. Relate this to the Pythagorean Theorem.

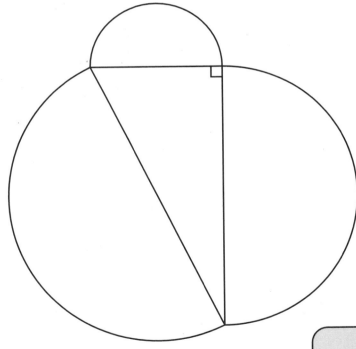

Rubric	
Writing focus	10
Construction	10
Area computation	10
Observations and relationship	20
TOTAL	**50**

Translating

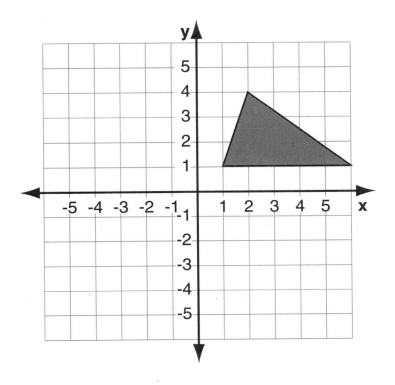

Type of Entry   Investigation/Discovery

Tools   Graph Paper, Ruler

Concepts   Space and Dimensionality, Change

Prompt   On graph paper, draw a triangle in the first quadrant. Label the coordinates of each vertex. Translate this triangle into the second quadrant and label the vertices. Reflect the original triangle into the fourth quadrant and label the vertices. Then show algebraically that all three of the triangles are congruent.

Rubric	
Writing focus	10
Graph	10
Algebraic congruence	10
Explanation	10
Concluding statements	10
TOTAL	**50**

Name _____ Date _____

What Am I?

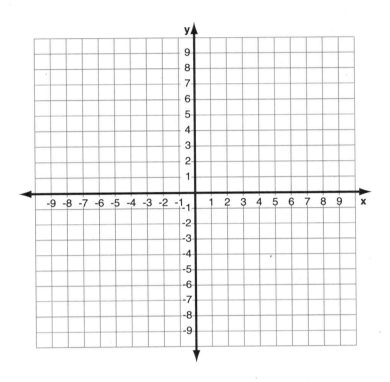

Type of Entry   Investigation/Discovery

Tools   Graph Paper, Ruler

Concepts   Mathematical Procedure, Space and Dimensionality,
Change, Measurement

Prompt   Choosing values for a, b, and c, construct a polygon with these points as
vertices: $(0,0)$, $(a,0)$, $(a+c,b)$, (c,b). Determine and show algebraically the
type of polygon formed.

Rubric	
Writing focus	10
Graph	10
Identification of polygon	10
Algebraic explanation	20
TOTAL	**50**

Name _____ Date _____

Jewelry Boxes

Type of Entry   Investigation/Discovery, Application

Concepts   Number, Mathematical Procedures, Space and Dimensionality, Measurement

Prompt   Joanne is designing boxes that will contain jewelry. She would like some of the boxes to have a volume of 72 cubic centimeters. If she uses only integers as dimensions for the edges, what are her possible dimensions? Would all of the boxes have an equal surface area? Which boxes would be practical for her use?

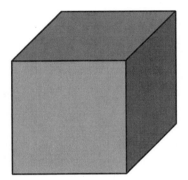

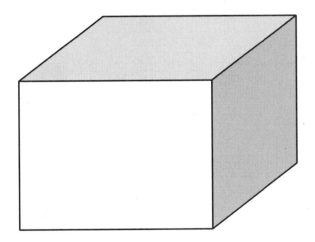

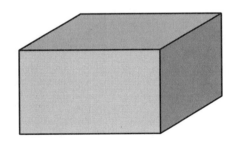

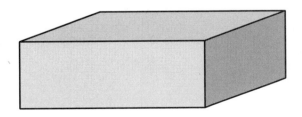

Rubric	
Writing focus	10
Solution of dimensions	10
Solution of surface area	10
Explanation	10
Conclusion	10
TOTAL	**50**

Name _____ Date _____

Tiling the Plane

Type of Entry Investigation/Discovery, Application

Tools Pattern Blocks

Concepts Space and Dimensionality, Change

Prompt Janey is picking out a new floor pattern for the kitchen. A polygon pattern will tile a plane if it will cover the plane with no spaces left uncovered. There are six polygons in a set of pattern blocks. Using these polygons, determine which of the six would tile the kitchen. Support your findings with an explanation or generalization about polygons that will tile the plane. Give a combination of pattern blocks that will tile. Using pattern blocks, make a pattern for the kitchen. Draw the pattern on a sheet of paper, covering the page, and color it.

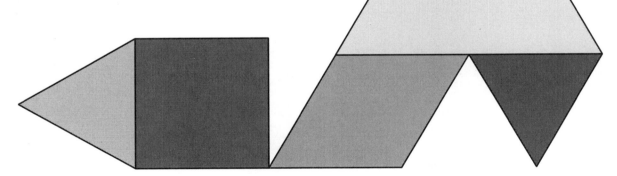

Rubric

Writing focus	10
Blocks that tile	10
Combinations that tile	10
Explanation of tiling	10
Floor pattern	10
TOTAL	**50**

A Round Peg in a Square Hole

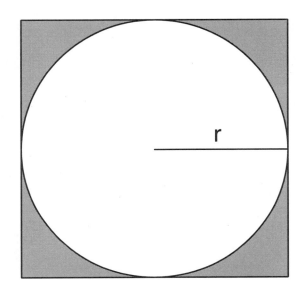 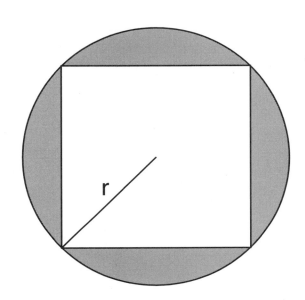

Type of Entry Investigation/Discovery

Concepts Mathematical Procedure, Space and Dimensionality, Measurement

Prompt Barbara wishes to determine whether it is better to be a "round peg in a square hole" or a "square hole in a round peg." Given the circle inscribed in a square and the square inscribed in a circle as shown above, which gives the larger interior area? How do the total areas compare? Which would you tell Barbara to pick and why?

Rubric	
Writing focus	10
Approach to problem	10
Formulas and calculations	10
Explanation	10
Conclusions	10
TOTAL	**50**

Isosceles Triangle Relationships

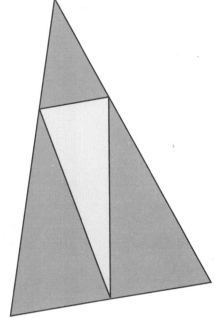

Type of Entry   Investigation/Discovery, Writing

Tools   Protractor, Compass, Ruler

Concepts   Mathematical Procedure, Change

Prompt   Draw several different sizes of isosceles triangles. Make two conjectures about isosceles triangles, giving some supporting evidence based on your measurements. Explain what led you to give each of your conjectures.

Rubric	
Writing focus	10
Drawings	10
Measurements and observations	10
Conjectures	10
Explanation	10
TOTAL	**50**

Name _____ Date _____

Midpoints of a Triangle

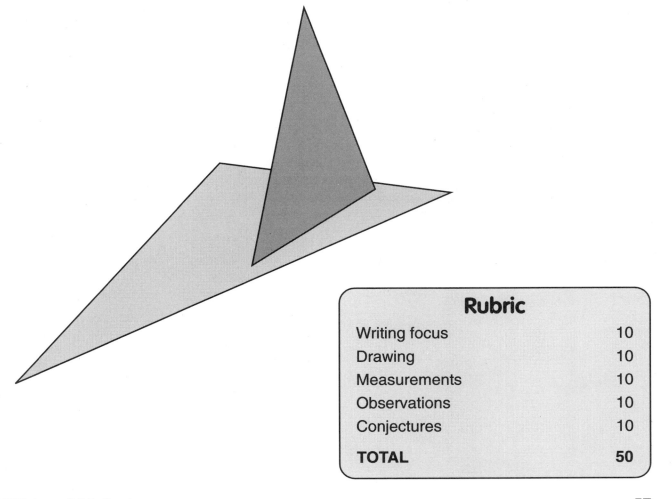

Type of Entry   Investigation/Discovery

Tools   Ruler, Protractor, Compass

Concepts   Space and Dimensionality, Measurement

Prompt   Draw a large scalene triangle. Locate the midpoints of the three sides. Connect the midpoints, forming a new triangle. Measure the parts of the triangles in the drawing and make two conjectures about this figure. Would your conjectures change if you used an isosceles triangle instead? If so, how?

Rubric	
Writing focus	10
Drawing	10
Measurements	10
Observations	10
Conjectures	10
TOTAL	**50**

The Mid-Segment

Type of Entry   Discovery/Investigation

Tools   Graph Paper, Ruler

Concepts   Number, Space and Dimensionality, Mathematical Procedures

Prompt   Using a sheet of graph paper, draw a triangle and label the coordinates of the vertices. Find the midpoint of two of the sides and draw a segment connecting them. There is a geometric theorem that states that this segment is parallel to the third side and also equal to half of its measure. Prove this theorem algebraically.

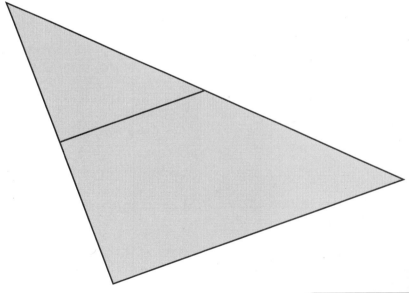

Rubric	
Writing focus	10
Graph	10
Formulas used	10
Calculations	10
Explanation	10
TOTAL	**50**

Name _____ Date _____

A Right Triangle

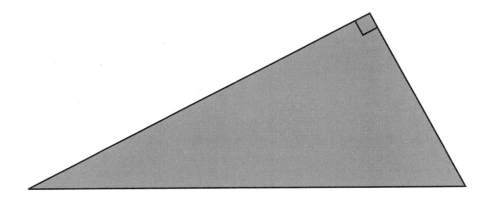

Type of Entry   Investigation/Discovery

Tools   Protractor, Ruler

Concepts   Mathematical Procedure, Measurement, Space and Dimensionality

Prompt   Draw a large right triangle on a sheet of paper, and draw the altitude from the right angle. Label each segment in your drawing with a different lowercase letter. Measure each part of your drawing. Compare the parts in each of the three triangles and generate a hypothesis regarding the triangles. Explain your hypothesis.

Rubric	
Writing focus	10
Drawing	10
Measurement accuracy	10
Hypothesis	10
Explanation	10
TOTAL	**50**

Landon's Number

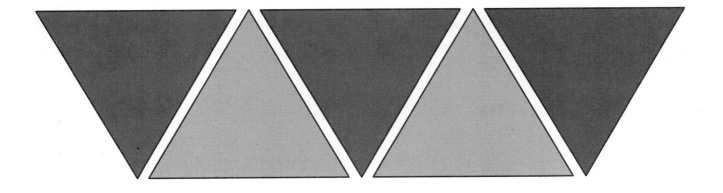

Type of Entry   Investigation/Discovery, Writing

Concepts   Number, Mathematical Procedures, Space and Dimensionality,
Measurement, Change, Mathematical Structure

Tools   Scientific Calculator

Prompt   Landon, wishing to avoid extra steps in calculation, has determined a
quick method to calculate the area of an equilateral triangle. He claims
that the product of the length of a side squared and the decimal .433 will
always give the area correct to the thousandths place. Show whether this
is true, and if so, why this would work with any equilateral triangle.

Rubric	
Writing focus	10
Approach to problem	10
Explanation	20
Conclusion	10
TOTAL	**50**

Name _____ Date _____

Rectangle Investigation

Type of Entry   Investigation/Discovery

Tools   Graph Paper, Ruler, Calculator, Compass, Protractor

Concepts   Measurement, Space and Dimensionality

Prompt   On a Cartesian coordinate system graph, draw a large nonsquare rectangle. Bisect each angle, extending the bisectors until they intersect all other bisectors in the diagram possible. Determine the type of geometric figure formed by all of these intersections. Substantiate your answer.

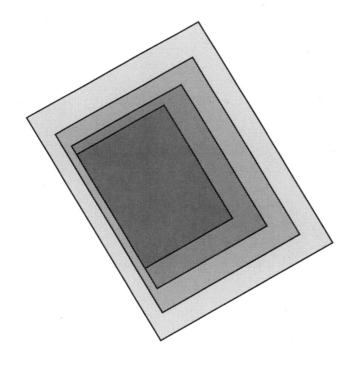

Rubric	
Writing focus	10
Drawing	10
Classification of polygon	10
Explanation	20
TOTAL	**50**

Name _____   Date _____

_____

_____

_____

_____

_____

_____

_____

_____

_____

_____

_____

_____

_____

_____

_____

_____

_____

_____

_____

_____

_____

_____

_____

_____

_____

Triangle Parallels

Type of Entry   Investigation/Discovery, Nonroutine

Tools   Ruler, Protractor

Concepts   Space and Dimensionality, Change, Mathematical Structure

Prompt   Draw 3 different types of triangles. Label each of the triangles *ABC*. On each triangle, place point *D* on *AC* (not at the midpoint) and draw *DP* parallel to *BC* with *P* on *AB*. Then draw *PR* parallel to *AC*. Draw *RX* parallel to *AB*, and continue drawing segments parallel to the sides and with all endpoints of the segments on the sides. What happens to the figure? Can you explain why this happens?

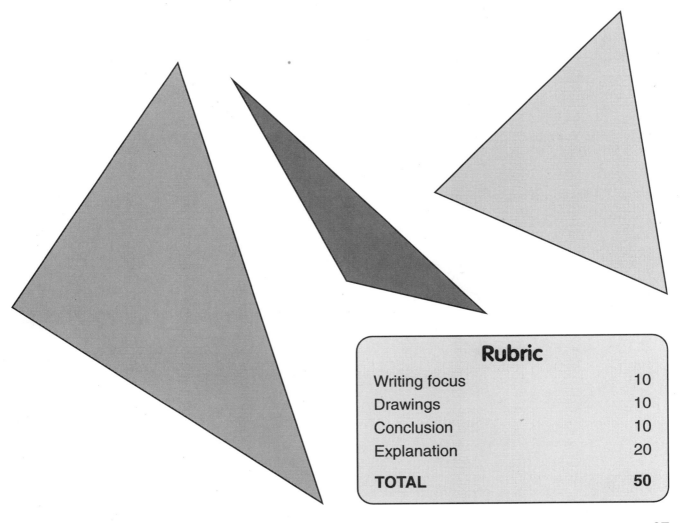

Rubric	
Writing focus	10
Drawings	10
Conclusion	10
Explanation	20
TOTAL	**50**

Name _____ Date _____

The Stick

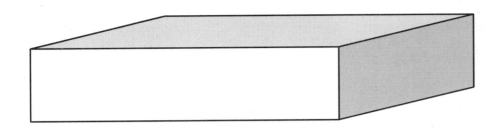

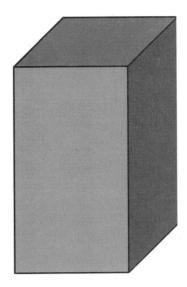

Type of Entry Investigation/Discovery, Application

Concepts Number, Mathematical Procedure, Space and Dimensionality, Measurement, Change

Prompt Anna has a riding crop that is 4 feet in length. She looks for a container so that she can hide the crop from her sister Sally. The box must have dimensions of at least 0.5 foot for each measurement, and the stick must fit diagonally across the box. What are the measurements of a box that would give the least and most volume? Which box would be most likely to fool Sally and why?

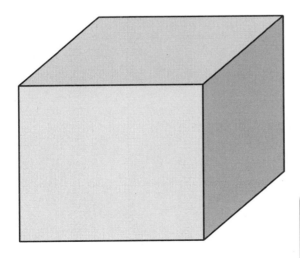

Rubric	
Writing focus	10
Drawings and charts	10
Explanation	10
Solution of measurements	10
Recommendation	10
TOTAL	**50**

Name _____ Date _____

The Hurricane

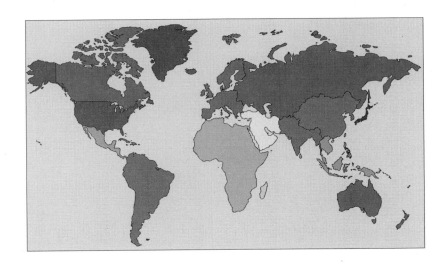

Type of Entry   Investigation/Discovery, Application

Tools   Ruler, Compass, Map, Protractor

Concepts   Space and Dimensionality, Measurement, Change

Prompt   John lives in Stuart, Florida, and is having a birthday party August 26th. Yesterday, August 24th, the weather channel reported on the formation of a hurricane, which was located equidistant from Jacksonville, Florida; Miami, Florida; and Sandy Point in the Bahamas. Today, 24 hours later, the hurricane is located equidistant from Sandy Point; Tampa, Florida; and Savannah, Georgia. Using the map on page 75, locate the center of the hurricane for each report. If the hurricane follows its present course, will it cause John's birthday party to be cancelled? (John will cancel the party if the hurricane comes within 100 miles of Stuart.)

Rubric	
Writing focus	10
Method of locating centers	10
Explanation of locations	10
Accuracy of drawing	10
Conclusion	10
TOTAL	**50**

Name _____   Date _____

Bermuda Triangle

Type of Entry Investigation/Discovery, Application

Concepts Date, Number, Measurement, Space and Dimensionality, Mathematical Procedure

Prompt Many ships and airplanes have disappeared in the area known as the "Bermuda Triangle" or the "Devil's Triangle." The area is generally considered to have vertices at Miami, Florida; Bermuda; and San Juan, Puerto Rico. David works in Miami and is in charge of air and sea rescue missions from that station. Using the map on page 76, figure the approximate area covered by the "Bermuda Triangle." Then plan a rescue mission for an airplane that was last heard from at the circumcenter of the triangle.

Rubric	
Writing focus	10
Calculation of area	20
Explanation of area	10
Construction of circumcenter	10
Calculation of circumcenter	20
Explanation of circumcenter	10
Rescue mission plan	20
TOTAL	**100**

The Hurricane Map

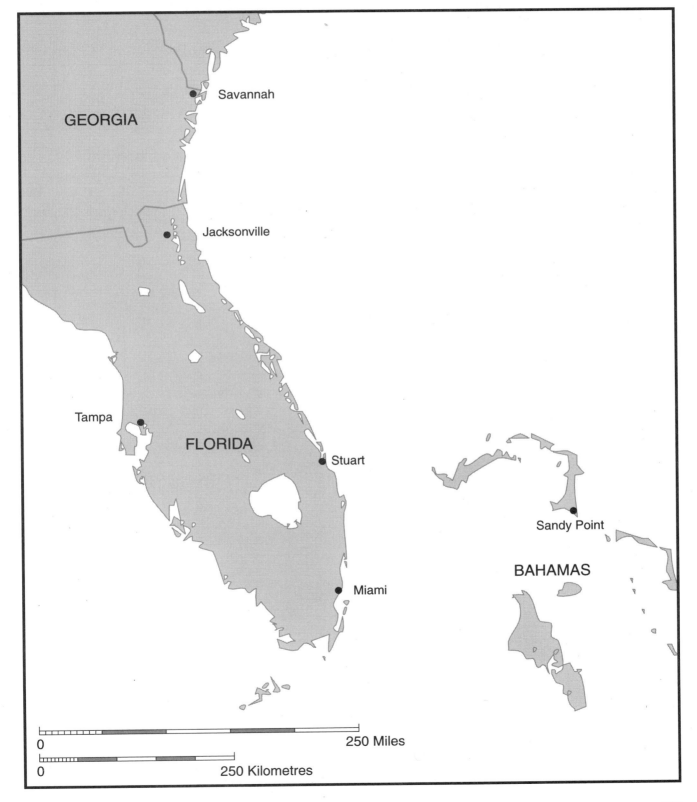

Bermuda Triangle Map

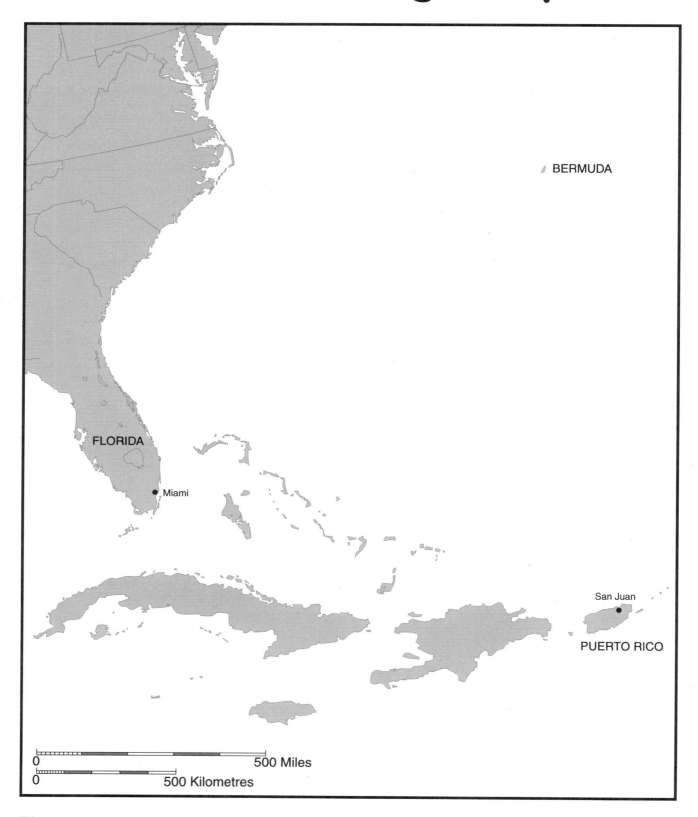

BERMUDA

FLORIDA

● Miami

San Juan
●

PUERTO RICO

0 ▭▭▭▭▭▭▭▭▭▭▭ 500 Miles
0 ▭▭▭▭▭▭▭▭▭▭▭ 500 Kilometres

Graph Area

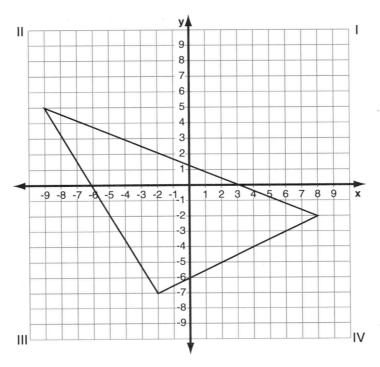

Type of Entry   Investigation/Discovery

Tools   Graph Paper, Ruler, Calculator

Concepts   Space and Dimensionality, Measurement, Mathematical Procedures

Prompt   On a Cartesian coordinate system, choose three points that are contained in three different quadrants. Using these as vertices of a triangle, find the area of the triangle using two different methods. Explain each method. Compare the two calculations.

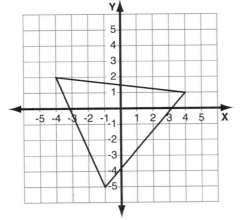

Rubric	
Writing focus	10
Complexity of point choice	10
Mathematics of methods	10
Explanation of methods used	10
Comparison of two forms	10
TOTAL	**50**

Name _____ Date _____

The Equation Story

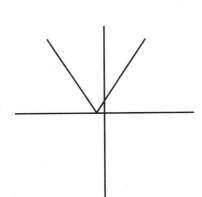

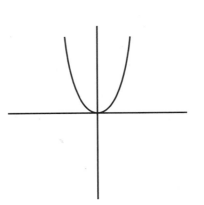

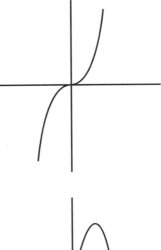

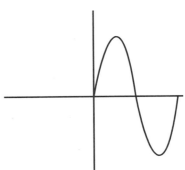

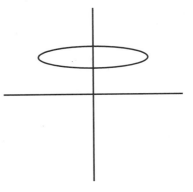

Type of Entry   Nonroutine, Project, Writing

Concepts   Change, Mathematical Structure

Prompt   Choose an equation that is not linear and contains at least two variables. Graph the equation. Make up a story, using this equation as the main character in your story. Make several changes in the numerical coefficients and constant and graph the changed equations to match your story. Incorporate the changed graphs into your story. Make a cover page and put your story in book form.

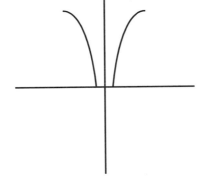

Rubric	
Writing focus	10
Cover page	20
Illustrations and graphs	20
Use of mathematics	20
Written story	20
Overall effort and effect	10
TOTAL	**100**

Name _____ Date _____

Graph Design

Type of Entry   Nonroutine, Writing, Project

Concepts   Space and Dimensionality, Change, Mathematical Structure

Prompt   Mathematics and art have many connections, such as proportion, perspective, symmetry, and beauty. These connections show up especially well in graphs. Design a work of art made up of the graphs of equations. Put the design on a sheet of graph paper, with all equations and restrictions shown beside the different parts. On another copy of the graph, color your design (and do not label equations, etc.). Write a paper explaining the types of equations used and how they were derived. Include any symmetries or transformations.

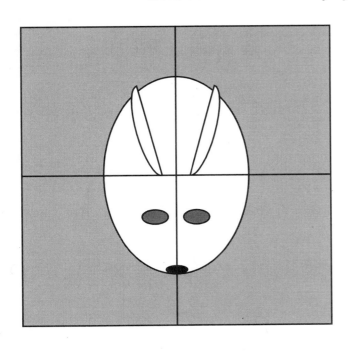

Rubric	
Writing focus	10
Equations and restrictions	20
Explanation of equations	20
Complexity	10
Finished product	20
Overall writing and conclusion	20
TOTAL	**100**

Framed!

Type of Entry   Investigation/Discovery, Application

Tools   Graphing Calculator, Graph Paper, Ruler

Concepts   Number, Space and Dimensionality, Measurement, Change

Prompt   Curt is matting some of his finished art pieces. He would like the border to be the same width all around the pictures. The finished size of one picture, including the frame, is 15" × 18". Set up an equation to show the relationship between the area inside the frame and the width of the border. Graph the equation on a graphing calculator and sketch it on graph paper. Explain how the graph relates to the picture. Using your trace on the graphing calculator, pick an area and determine the width of the border at that area. Which width would you choose for the picture?

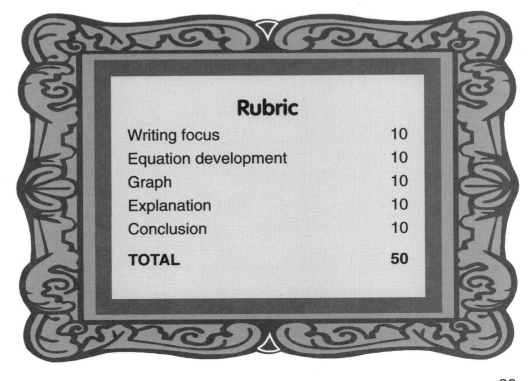

Rubric

Writing focus	10
Equation development	10
Graph	10
Explanation	10
Conclusion	10
TOTAL	**50**

Simon Says

Type of Entry   Nonroutine, Application

Tools   Graphing Calculator (optional), Graph Paper

Concepts   Number, Mathematical Procedure, Space and Dimensionality, Change, Measurement

Prompt   Beth is planning a birthday party for Caleb and his friends Eli and Luke. As an avid mathematics student, Beth has determined a different way to play "Simon Says." She places everyone in a line and then walks 1,280 steps from the starting line. Every time someone has "Simon's" permission to advance, that person must step off half the distance between him or her and the finish line. In order to win, a person must have less than half a step left. Set up an equation and a graph to show this relationship. At which $f(x)$ would a person be a winner? How would the game be affected if a person could win only if he or she covered the entire distance? Suppose your graph included times when "Simon" didn't say?

Rubric

Writing focus	10
Equation	10
Graph	10
Explanation	10
Conclusion	10
TOTAL	**50**

Name _____ Date _____

Grid Changes

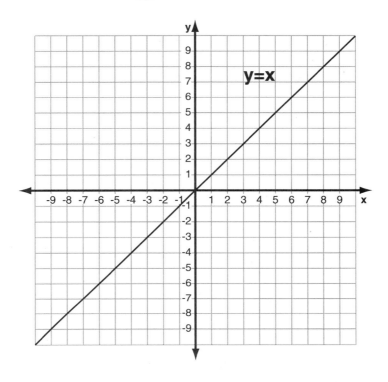

y=x

Type of Entry   Investigation/Discovery, Writing

Tools   Graphing Calculator (optional)

Concepts   Mathematical Procedure, Space and Dimensionality, Change, Mathematical Structure

Prompt   Donna and Sue Ellen are discussing the effect of "doubling" an equation. Sue Ellen claims that if $y = x$ looks like the graph above, then $y = 2x$ would look the same, except that it would be twice as long. Donna, after explaining that the graph extends beyond the area shown, uses several examples to show the "doubling" effect. Pick three equations, including at least one nonlinear equation, and "double" them. Then graph and summarize the effect of "doubling" them.

Rubric	
Writing focus	10
Complexity of problems	10
Graphs	10
Observations and patterns	10
Conclusion	10
TOTAL	**50**

Green Paint

Type of Entry   Investigation/Discovery, Application

Concepts   Number, Measurement, Change, Mathematical Procedure

Prompt   Harold and Susan are remodeling. They have two containers of 100 ml each of paint, one yellow and one blue. They wish to mix the paint to obtain a green color, but each container will hold only 150 ml. Harold, always liking a challenge, proposes to mix them using only the two containers. Susan states that all he has to do is put 50 ml of yellow into the blue, mix it, and return 50 ml of the mixture to the yellow container. Harold says that would not work. Who is correct and why? If Susan is incorrect, how could Harold solve the problem?

Rubric	
Writing focus	10
Illustration of problem	10
Mathematical approach	10
Explanation	10
Conclusion	10
TOTAL	**50**

Name _____ Date _____

Area/Volume

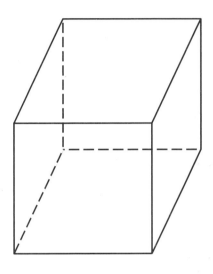
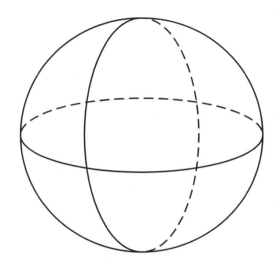

Type of Entry   Investigation/Discovery, Writing

Tools   Graph Paper, Graphing Calculator (optional)

Concepts   Space and Dimensionality, Change, Measurement

Prompt   Set up equations for the surface area and the volume of a sphere. Graph them on the same graph. Then do the same for a cube, using a separate graph. Compare the area and volume graphs for each of the solids, and also draw a conclusion comparing the cube and the sphere.

Rubric	
Writing focus	10
Equations	10
Graphs of equations	10
Comparison of the equations on each graph	10
Conclusion	10
TOTAL	**50**

Name _____ Date _____

Animal Cookies

Type of Entry Investigation/Discovery, Application

Tools One Die

Concepts Number, Mathematical Procedure, Mathematical Structure, Data

Prompt Dylan really likes the animal cookies that his mom, Jill, buys for him. There are six different types of animals in the box. Dylan wants to eat all six kinds each time he is allowed to have the cookies. Although the cookies are small, Jill doesn't want to let him eat too many at a time. What is the probable number of cookies she could expect him to take in order to get all six different kinds if he "grabs" them randomly? Set up a means of testing this concept using a die.

Rubric	
Writing focus	10
Probability	10
Explanation of probability	10
Test with die	10
Results and conclusion	10
TOTAL	**50**

Name _____ Date _____

Pascal's Patterns

Type of Entry   Investigation/Discovery

Concepts   Number, Mathematical Procedure, Change, Mathematical Structure

Prompt   Using Pascal's Triangle on page 97, shade in two rows or lines of numbers. Describe the pattern shown in the numbers and determine an equation for the pattern. If the pattern is not a set of horizontal numbers, give the next number in that sequence.

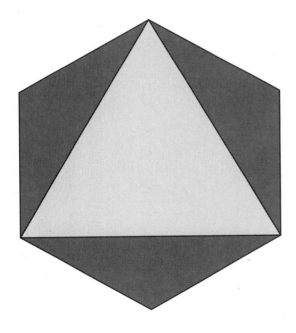

Rubric	
Writing focus	10
Description of patterns	10
Equations	10
Explanation	10
Pattern choice and final numbers	10
TOTAL	**50**

Pascal's Triangle

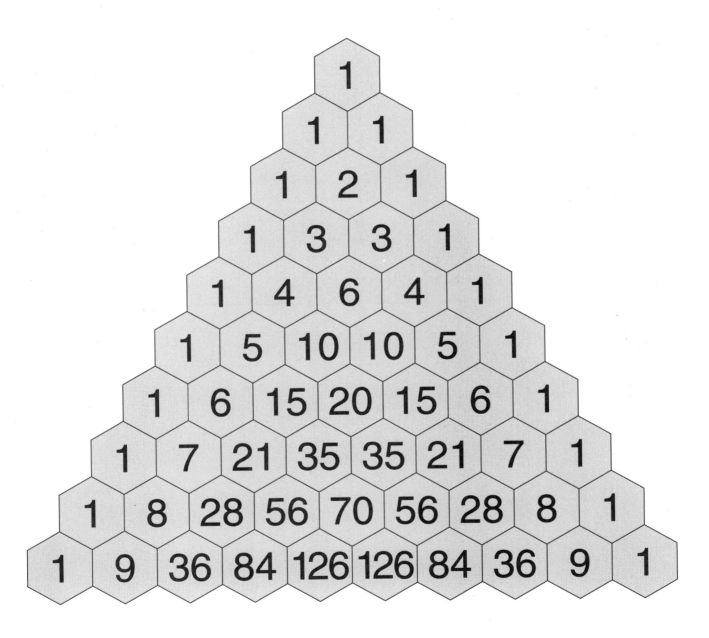

I.D. Code

Jane Doe	?????????????
John Doe	?????????????

Type of Entry Investigation/Discovery, Application

Concepts Number, Change, Mathematical Structure, Data

Prompt Wisdom University is designing an I.D. code for all students. The officials do not want the code to be unnecessarily long. However, they want to be able to assign a different code to each student. In order to avoid duplication, they would like to project a different code for each student for the next 50 years. They would also like to build into their code a classification for male and female in order to facilitate dormitory assignments. The present enrollment of the university is around 10,000 students. Determine a method for designing the code, and give the total number of students that could be assigned using your code.

Rubric	
Writing focus	10
Approach to the problem	10
Classification system	10
Explanation of system	10
Conclusion	10
TOTAL	**50**

Shadow Change

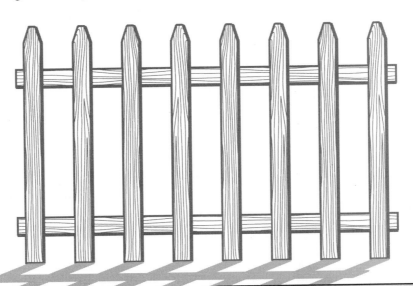

Type of Entry   Investigation/Discovery, Project

Tools   Measuring Tape or Meter Stick, Fixed Object

Concepts   Measurement, Change, Mathematical Structure, Data

Prompt   On a sunny day, measure the length of the shadow of a fixed object, such as a post, for each hour of daylight. Set up the information in a chart and graph the information on a Cartesian graph. Graph the function over a 24-hour period. Make a graph projecting over a 72-hour period. Can you find a function that might fit your graph? Do you think the graph would change if you gathered your data 6 months from this time?

Rubric	
Writing focus	10
Data chart	10
Graphs	10
Discussion	10
Conclusion	10
TOTAL	**50**

Name _____   Date _____

Parabola Area

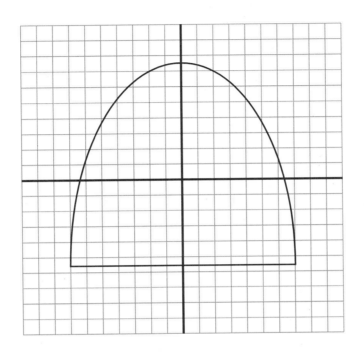

Type of Entry   Investigation/Discovery, Nonroutine

Tools   Graphing Calculator, Graph Paper

Concepts   Number, Space and Dimensionality, Measurement, Change, Mathematical Structure

Prompt   Graph the two equations $y = x^2 - 6$, and $y = -3x^2 - 2x + 8$ on a sheet of graph paper. Using your geometric knowledge of area, find an approximate area between the graphs of the equations using the two intersection points as boundaries. Then see if you can develop another means of finding that area.

Rubric	
Writing focus	10
Graph of equations	10
Geometric area	10
Second means for area	10
Conclusion	10
TOTAL	**50**

Air Crash!

Type of Entry   Investigation/Discovery

Tools   Compass, Protractor, Graph Paper, Calculator, Ruler

Concepts   Number, Space and Dimensionality, Change, Measurement, Mathematical Procedures

Prompt   Tom is over point A at 10:00 A.M. flying at 300 m.p.h. in a direction of 60 degrees west of north. At 11:00 A.M. Dick flies over point B, 1500 miles due west of point A. Dick is flying at 250 m.p.h. in a direction of 45 degrees east of north. If they continue at the same speed in the directions they are headed, flying at the same altitude, how close will they come to each other? At what time will they be closest?

Rubric	
Writing focus	10
Graph of flights	10
Explanation	10
Calculations	10
Conclusion	10
TOTAL	**50**

Name _____ Date _____

© NTC/Contemporary Publishing Group, Inc.

Egg-zackly

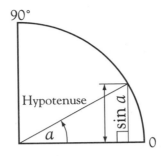

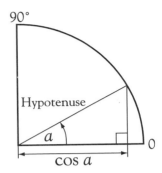

Type of Entry   Nonroutine, Writing, Group Project

Tools   Scientific Calculator, Graph Paper, Ruler

Concepts   Number, Mathematical Procedures, Measurement, Space and Dimensionality

Prompt   John is having an Easter egg hunt for Eddie and his friends. In order to find the prize egg, they must follow his directions. Since Eddie is quite precocious for his age, the directions John gives must be calculated using the trigonometric functions of sine, cosine, and tangent. Draw your path on a sheet of graph paper and then give your directions, using the path on your graph as your map. (For example: Beginning at point A, walk north 10 meters, then turn and walk east to point B, which is 25 degrees east of north from point A.) Make a copy of your map. Determine all distances needed. Then go out to a football field or some other appropriate location and walk off your directions. Bury your prize egg. Test your map and directions by giving them to another group and observing the group as they calculate and look for the prize egg. How successful were they? Write a group report and an individual report on the project.

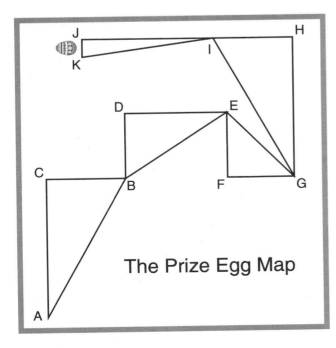

The Prize Egg Map

Rubric	
Writing focus	10
Uncalculated map	10
Written directions	20
Calculated map	10
Group test (validity)	10
Group observations	20
Individual write-up	20
TOTAL	**100**

Circle the Ellipse

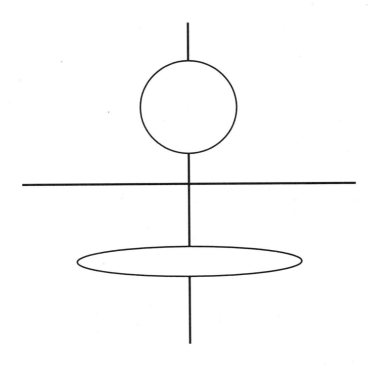

Type of Entry   Investigation/Discovery, Writing

Concepts   Number, Space and Dimensionality, Mathematical Structure, Change

Prompt   The equations for a circle and an ellipse are similar, since a circle is a specialized ellipse. The formulas for the area of each are also similar. Pick a value for r in the circle, and then compare the formula and area of the circle with 2 ellipses of the same area. How would you generate ellipses with the same area as a given circle?

Rubric

Writing focus	10
Approach to the problem	10
Comparison of formulas	10
Explanation of problem	10
Conclusion	10
TOTAL	**50**

Cycling

Type of Entry   Investigation/Discovery, Application

Tools   Stopwatch or Watch with Second Hand, Graphing Calculator

Concepts   Number, Mathematical Procedures, Change, Measurement

Prompt   Dana is training for a bicycle race and Jim is timing her. He is a coach and a mathematics teacher, so he decides to time her as she finishes each lap. Choose someone who is a conditioned cyclist or runner and time him or her riding or running laps. Using a graphing calculator, plot these points. Determine the line of best fit. Discuss the type of equation and make a prediction for an additional number of laps covered.

Rubric	
Writing focus	10
Data and graph	10
Equation	10
Explanation	10
Conclusion	10
TOTAL	**50**

3-V

Dick and Jane and Spot are going on a picnic. They are taking . . .

Type of Entry   Investigation/Discovery, Application, Nonroutine

Tools   Graphing Calculator (optional)

Concepts   Number, Mathematical Procedures, Change, Mathematical Structure

Prompt   Algebraic systems may be displayed and solved in a variety of ways. Using Venn diagrams, matrices, graphs, or equations. Make up a word problem in three variables. Show and explain the solution of the problem in two different ways.

Rubric	
Writing focus	10
Word problem	10
Types of solutions	10
Explanations	10
Complexity of problem	10
TOTAL	**50**

Name _____ Date _____

The Roof

Type of Entry   Investigation/Discovery, Application

Tools   Scientific Calculator, Graph Paper, Ruler

Concepts   Number, Mathematical Procedures, Space and Dimensionality, Measurement, Change

Prompt   Tony and Whit are putting a roof on the house they are building. On the back of the house there is a 6-foot-wide porch area. The slope of the roof on the porch area is 2 inches to 1 foot, and the slope of the roof on the house is 4 inches to 1 foot. How long do they need to make the rafters that run from the edge of the porch to the roof of the house? They can pitch the roof of the house anywhere from 4 to 5 inches to the foot. How would changing the pitch of the roof affect the length of the porch rafters?

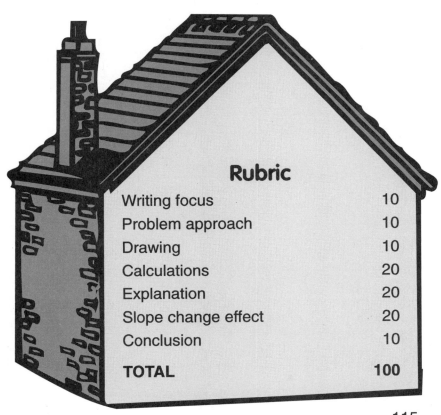

Rubric

Writing focus	10
Problem approach	10
Drawing	10
Calculations	20
Explanation	20
Slope change effect	20
Conclusion	10
TOTAL	**100**

Name _____ Date _____

The Dart Game

Type of Entry   Investigation/Discovery, Nonroutine, Application

Concepts   Number, Mathematical Procedures, Space and Dimensionality, Measurement, Data

Prompt   Brenda and Chris are making their own dart game. Chris, an innovative mathematics student, designs a dart board as shown on page 121, with the length of the radius of the large circle divided equally by each figure when it is perpendicular to the sides of the squares. What is the probability that a dart that hits the board will score if only the darkened parts count? Suppose that the inner circle is worth 5 points, the light inner square is worth 4 points, the dark middle circle is worth 3 points, the outer light square part is worth 2 points, and the outer dark circle part 1 point. If each team could choose either dark or light, with points coming only from their areas, which choice would be the better one?

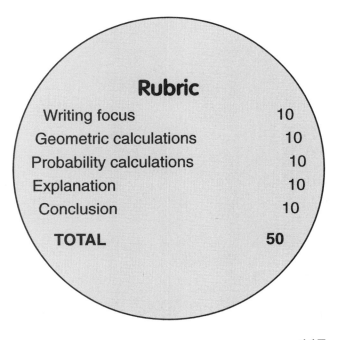

Rubric

Writing focus	10
Geometric calculations	10
Probability calculations	10
Explanation	10
Conclusion	10
TOTAL	**50**

Fractal Area

Type of Entry   Writing, Investigation/Discovery

Tools   Graphing Calculator (optional)

Concepts   Number, Mathematical Procedures, Change, Mathematical Structure, Space and Dimensionality

Prompt   Using the drawing on page 122, or creating a fractal of your own, assign a length to the sides in the original figure. Develop a formula for finding the area of the figure. Determine the area of the fractal as the number of additions approaches infinity. Explain your solution.

F
R
A
C
T
A
L

F
R A
A C T A
C T
L

Rubric	
Writing focus	10
Area formulas	10
Calculations	10
Explanation	10
Conclusion	10
TOTAL	**50**

Name _____ Date _____

Dart Game Board

Square Fractal

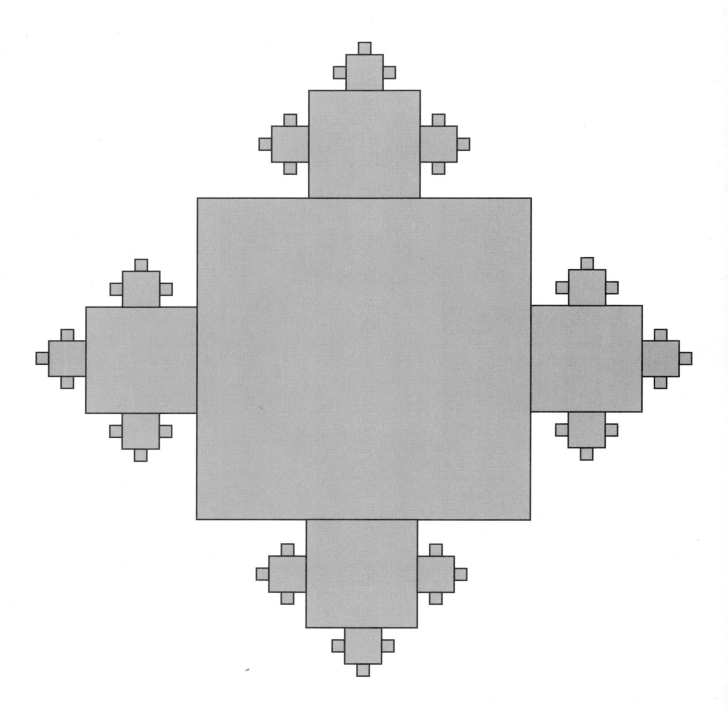

Corn and Hay

Type of Entry   Investigation/Discovery, Application

Tools   Graphing Calculator, Graph Paper, Ruler

Concepts   Number, Measurement, Change, Mathematical Structure

Prompt   Williamson Stables wishes to determine the correct feeding quantities for its mares. According to Morrison's Feeding Standards, a 1000-pound mare requires 13 to 16 pounds of dry matter per day and 0.7 to 0.8 pound of digestible protein. Number-one-grade corn is 87% dry matter and 6.9% protein, and mixed hay is 88.2% dry matter and 4.5% protein. Using a linear program approach, calculate the optimum required amount of hay and corn necessary for this mare for one day. If hay sells for $2.50 per 50-pound bale and corn is $8.00 per 100 pounds, how much would it cost to feed one mare for an average 30-day month?

Rubric	
Writing focus	10
Overall approach	10
Equations	20
Graphs	20
Explanation	20
Solution	20
TOTAL	**100**